Everyday

Daniel Diet Cookbook

Quick and Easy Recipes for the Entire Family

Disclaimer

What Will You Find in This Book?

The Daniel Diet is a biblical way of leading your life. The everyday life has become so busy that people find it hard to take out time from their busy schedules and focus on God. To overcome this problem, Daniel Diet has come up with a fasting method, through which a person can get closer to God and build a strong relationship.

To make sure that at the end of a fast, a person is able to cleanse spiritually, the plan also provides some of the most brilliant recipes, which are not only healthy but also fulfilling. By following the plan, you will not only be able to lead a healthy life but also one, which is based on biblical principles.

Reading this book will help you in creating recipes, which are spiritually fit to be used, while fasting and afterwards as well. In this book, you will find Daniel Diet recipes, which are healthy, tasty, and full of nutrition. So without further ado, let us find out what those recipes are and start cooking!

Table of Contents

Everyday

Daniel Diet Cookbook

Quick and Easy Recipes for the Entire Family

These Recipes are so effective that more and more people have started opting for them. Try out the recipes provided in the book, and test your culinary skills, while creating phenomenal meals for your friends and family.

Apple and Oats Porridge

SERVES 4

Prep Time: 10 minutes

Cooking Time: 10 minutes

Nutritional Facts:

Calories 201

Total Fat 2g

Carbohydrates 43g

Protein 4g

Ingredients

4 cups of water

Soy milk (optional)

1 ½ cups of oat barn

1 apple (large, cored, peeled and diced)

½ teaspoon of ground caraway seeds

½ teaspoon of cinnamon

1/3 cup of raisins

½ teaspoon of salt

Directions

Take a deep saucepan and heat water in it on high heat. Bring the water to boil and then add in the oats. Stir the oats while they cook, and then let the water boil again. Once the water comes to boil, bring the heat down to low, and allow the oats to cook for an additional two minutes. Make sure to give it an occasional stir. Turn off the heat, and remove the saucepan after two minutes and then add in the raisins, spices, and apples.

Serve

Mix it thoroughly to combine all the ingredients evenly and then leave them for 5 minutes to combine all of the flavors. Once ready, transfer to a serving bowl, serve with milk (optional) and enjoy!

Potato and Green Onion Frittata

SERVES 4

Prep Time: 10 minutes

Cooking Time: 20 minutes

Nutritional Facts:

Calories 281

Total Fat 13.1g

Carbohydrates 28.7g

Protein 12.5g

Ingredients

¼ cup of olive oil

1 onion (finely chopped)

2 lbs tofu (firm)

5 green onions (finely chopped)

2 potatoes (medium, shredded)

2 teaspoon of salt

4 garlic cloves (finely chopped)

½ teaspoon of pepper (freshly ground)

2-3 tablespoon of soy sauce

Method

Place a large skillet and heat a little bit of olive oil in it on medium heat. Once the oil is hot, add in the white bits of the green onions only and the onions and cook them for 2-3 minutes or until they start becoming soft and translucent.

Then add in the garlic and sauté it for half a minute. Add in around ¼ teaspoon of pepper, 1 teaspoon of salt and potatoes before increasing the heat to high. Allow the potatoes to cook for 10-15 minutes, making sure to stir and flip the potatoes so that they are golden brown in color from all sides.

In a blender add in the soy sauce, remaining pepper and salt, along with the tofu and blend it together until the mixture is smooth and creamy. Mix the green part of the finely chopped green onions in this mixture and then pour it over the potato mix in the skillet.

Transfer this mixture into a greased baking pan and let it bake in a preheated oven with its temperature set at 350°F for 30-40 minutes or until the frittata is set firmly.

Serve

Take it out of the oven; allow it to cool, before serving it warm. Enjoy!

Vegetable Soup

SERVES 4

Prep Time: 20 minutes

Cooking Time: 50 minutes

Nutritional Facts:

Calories 116

Total Fat 0.6g

Carbohydrates 24.3g

Protein 4g

Ingredients

2 tablespoons of olive oil

2 cups of onions (finely chopped)

8 cups of mixed frozen vegetables (diced)

1 cup of celery (finely sliced)

Salt and Pepper (as required)

3 cans of vegetables broth (14.5 oz)

1 can of tomato (diced and drained, 28 oz)

2 teaspoons of Italian seasoning

2 tablespoons of tomato paste

Directions

Take a large pot and on medium heat, drizzle a little bit of oil in it, allowing the oil to heat up. Then add in the celery, and onions, along with the Italian seasoning and then mix them all thoroughly together.

Add pepper and salt, as required and then allow the mixture to cook, until the onions start to soften and become translucent. This will take around 5-8 minutes. Pour in the vegetable broth, add in the tomatoes along with their juice and then the tomato paste, mix it thoroughly and then add 3 cups of water. Bring the mixture to a boil and then turn the heat down to low. Let the concoction simmer for 20 minutes on low.

After this, add in the mixed vegetables, then cover with a lid, and let the soup cook for 20-25 minutes.

Serve

Taste and adjust the seasoning, if necessary, and then allow the soup to cool for a couple of minutes before pouring in a blender and pulsing until it is a smooth mixture. Transfer back to the pot, allow it to heat up, and then serve hot. Enjoy!

Carrot and Ginger Soup

SERVES 4

Prep Time: 15 minutes

Cooking Time: 55 minutes

Nutritional Facts:

Calories 116

Total Fat 0.6g

Carbohydrates 24.3g

Protein 4g

Ingredients

1.5 lbs. of carrots (chopped and diced)

1 zucchini (chopped, peeled, and diced)

1 onion (chopped)

1 tablespoon of olive oil

3 cups of vegetable broth

1 liter of water

3 cloves of garlic

Raw ginger (according to taste)

Cinnamon (according to taste)

Cumin (according to taste)

Black pepper (according to taste)

Salt (according to taste

Directions

Take a large pot and sauté the ginger and onion in olive oil until for 3-5 minutes or until they start to soften over high heat.

When the garlic and onion soften, add the vegetable broth and the carrots and bring the heat down to medium. Bring to a boil then allow to simmer for 40 minutes or until the carrots have softened. Season the soup with cinnamon, cumin and black pepper and salt and raw ginger according to taste.

Let the soup cool down a bit before using a food processor to blend and smoothen the soup. For a chunkier consistency, hold back one or two cups of unblended soup and mix it in with the smooth one.

Serve

Serve with a dollop of yogurt or sour cream if desired and enjoy!

Artichoke Vinaigrette with Green Salad
SERVES 8

Prep Time: 15 minutes

Cooking Time: 30 minutes

Nutritional Value per Serving:

Calories: 112

Carbohydrates: 6g

Total Fat: 9g

Protein: 2g

Ingredients

3 tablespoons of fresh lemon juice

1/3 cup of extra virgin olive oil

1 packet of mixed greens (2-5 ounce)

1 jar of Artichoke hearts (12 ounce, drained and roughly chopped)

Salt and Pepper (according to taste)

Method:

Whisk the oil, salt, pepper and lemon juice in a medium sized bowl. Slowly add in the chopped artichoke hearts and whisk until they're well coated with the vinaigrette. Take out the mixed greens and prepare according to the instructions on the packet.

Serve:

Divide the greens into equal portions on each plate. Top off with the prepared artichoke vinaigrette and serve cold.

Arugula, Apple and Creamy Barley Salad
SERVES 4

Prep Time: 15 minutes

Cooking Time: 35 minutes

Nutritional Value per Serving:

Calories: 198

Carbohydrates: 2g

Total Fat: 8g

Protein: 5g

Ingredients

½ cup of yogurt (low fat, plain)

½ cup of pearl barley

1 tablespoon of fresh lemon juice

1 teaspoon of Dijon mustard

2 tablespoons of extra virgin olive oil

¼ cup of fresh mint (chopped, optional)

6 cups of Arugula (stems removed)

1 apple (thinly sliced)

2 celery stalks (sliced)

Salt and Pepper (according to taste)

Method:

Take a pot of water, add salt to it and let it come to a boil on medium heat. Add the barley and reduce the heat to low. Cover and let it simmer for 25 to 30 minutes or until the barley is tender and the water is largely absorbed. Set aside and drain on the baking sheet. Leave to cool.

Whisk the mustard, lemon juice, oil, and yogurt with some salt and pepper in a large bowl. Add apples and the barley and toss the salad thoroughly.

Serve

Serve warm with the creamy barley and apple salad added on top of the arugula on the bowls and

Pecan and Orange Salad
SERVES 8

Prep Time: 15 minutes

Cooking Time: 30 minutes

Nutritional Value per Serving:

Calories: 159

Carbohydrates: 8g

Total Fat: 14g

Protein: 3g

Ingredients

3 heads of lettuce

2 oranges (de-seeded, skinned and sliced into thin circles)

¾ cup of pecans (toasted and roughly chopped)

¼ cup of orange juice

1 shallot (minced)

1 tablespoon of white wine vinegar

¼ cup of extra olive oil

Salt and Pepper (according to taste)

Method:

Mix the oranges, the lettuce and the pecans in a large bowl.

In a separate bowl place the olive oil, vinegar, shallot, orange juice, salt and pepper and whisk together. Add this to the salad and toss thoroughly before serving.

Serve:

Serve cold. Use the lettuce leaf to make rolls and spoon the other vegetables in it. You can also lay a few lettuce leaves and spoon the salad out on top of them, using them as plates.

Dill Hash and Smoked Salmon with Fried Eggs

SERVES 4

Prep Time: 20 minutes

Cooking Time: 25 minutes

Nutritional Value per Serving:

Calories: 400

Carbohydrates: 42g

Total Fat: 16g

Protein: 21g

Ingredients

2 tablespoons of olive oil

1 ½ pound of Yukon gold potatoes (skinned and diced into ¼ inch cubes)

1 cup of onion (chopped)

4 ounces of salmon (flaked and smoked)

2 tablespoons of sour cream

2 teaspoons of Horse Radish (prepared/store bought)

1 teaspoon of Dijon mustard

2 tablespoons of chives (chopped)

1 tablespoon of fresh parsley (minced)

2 Eggs (optional)

Salt and Pepper (according to taste)

Lemon wedges (according to taste)

Extra sour cream (according to taste)

Method:

Take a large saucepan and heat some oil in it. Add potatoes, onions and garnish them all with some salt and pepper. Cook for 15- 20 minutes or until the potatoes start to brown. Keep stirring them every 2-3 minutes and to check them for softness.

Set the potatoes and onions aside. Take a large bowl and mix all the salmon, chives, Dijon mustard, sour cream, parsley and horse radish together. Once you're sure that the potatoes are cooked, turn off the heat and fold in the salmon mixture thoroughly and set it aside, allowing it to cook in residual heat of the pan for 5 minutes.

Serve:

Serve hot and you can serve with a runny fried egg on the side with some lemon juice sprinkled on top and a healthy dollop of sour cream to go along with the rest. Eggs are optional though, you can also remove it from the recipe if you like.

Honey Butter Sweet Potatoes

SERVES 1

Prep Time: 15 minutes

Cooking Time: 30 minutes

Nutritional Value per Serving:

Calories: 163

Carbohydrates: 26g

Total Fat: 6g

Protein: 2g

Ingredients

2 sweet potatoes (14 pounds, skinned and cut)

6 tablespoons of butter (¾ stick of butter)

3 tablespoons of honey

1 teaspoon of fresh lemon juice

Salt and Pepper (according to taste)

Method:

Preheat the oven to 350F. In a saucepan, combine the butter, the honey and the lemon juice together. On medium heat, stir the ingredients together until the butter melts and you get a smooth sauce ready.

Use a baking tray, grease it with some butter, and layer the sweet potatoes it. Pour the butter mixture over the sweet potatoes and give them a good toss to make sure that they are coated completely with the butter mixture. Add on a good pinch of salt and pepper and let them bake in the oven for 30 minutes or until you put a fork in the potatoes and it feels tender to you.

Serve:

These make an excellent meal or snack. Serve hot or cold. You can also serve them with some extra honey drizzled on top. If you like, you can also spoon some delicious almond butter or hazelnut butter to have with the baked potatoes.

Portobello Mushroom Caps with Baked Eggs and Prosciutto
SERVES 3-4

Prep Time: 30 minutes

Cooking Time: 30 minutes

Nutritional Value per Serving:

Calories: 114

Carbohydrates: 17g

Total Fat: 4g

Protein: 2g

Serving Size: 3 or 4

Ingredients

6 Portobello mushroom caps

6 strips of Prosciutto

6 fresh eggs

1 teaspoon of fresh parsley (chopped, can also use thyme instead)

3 tablespoons of olive oil

Salt and Pepper (according to taste)

Method:

First of all, make sure to prepare your Portobello mushroom caps. Remove the stem, wipe them clean and scrape out their gills so that the mushroom caps resemble small bowl like shapes.

When you've cleaned your mushroom caps, apply a bit of olive oil on the outside of the caps so that they'll cook more easily and won't stick to the baking paper.

Line a baking tray with baking paper and place the mushroom caps on it. Take one slice of prosciutto and line the inside of the mushroom cap with it. Make sure that the prosciutto slice fits inside the mushroom cap even if you have to fold it into the cap.

Once all your mushroom caps have been stuffed with prosciutto, crack an egg in to a small bowl or a teacup and very carefully, slide or pour the egg into the Portobello mushroom cap. Be very careful since a large egg yolk would make the mushroom cap over-turn or cause the egg to spill out on its own and you will have to try again after you clean up the mess.

Once you've got all the eggs in their mushroom caps, season them on top with some pepper and fresh parsley or thyme. Go easy on the salt since prosciutto happens to be a rather salty meat and adding extra salt might make it unbearably salty for you.

After seasoning all the eggs, lift the baking tray and extremely carefully put the mushroom caps in the oven. Be extremely gentle to avoid upsetting any mushroom caps. Once they're in the oven, let them cook for 30 minutes or until you feel the mushroom cap and egg are cooked to your liking

Let them cool for 5- 10 minutes before you take them out of the oven.

Serve:

Serve hot with a sour cream and dill dip to add. You can also use the mushroom caps as a great side dish for BBQ's, steaks or roast dinners or have them alone.

Quinoa Pilaf with Cod Fillets and Broccoli

SERVES 4

Prep Time: 25 minutes

Cooking Time: 45 minutes

Nutritional Value per Serving:

Calories: 464

Carbohydrates: 44g

Total Fat: 16g

Protein: 37g

Ingredients

1 cup of quinoa (rinsed well)

½ an onion (small, chopped)

3 tablespoons of olive oil

2 cups of broccoli (chopped)

¼ cup of raisins

½ cup of almonds (roasted, chopped coarsely)

4 fillets of Cod (6 ounces, skinless, de-boned)

2 scallions (sliced)

Salt and Pepper (according to taste)

Method:

In a large bowl, season the cod fillets with salt, pepper and paprika and set aside to let them marinate a bit before you cook them.

Take a skillet and on medium, heat a tablespoon of the oil. Add the onions and cook them in it for 3-4 minutes or longer, depending on how fast they cook. Season them with some salt and pepper and cook until the onions begin to turn brown and show signs of caramelization.

Take a deep bottomed pan and our 1 ½ cup of water in it. Add the quinoa in it and bring it up to a boil and then let it simmer down before covering it and letting it cook like that for 10 to 12 minutes or until you can see that almost all the water is gone.

Now take the lid off and fold the raisins and the chopped broccoli into the quinoa and let them cook for another 10 to 8 minutes or until the broccoli and quinoa is tender to the touch. When they feel tender, take them off from the heat and fold in the scallions and almonds and season with some salt and pepper before setting them aside.

Take the remaining two tablespoons of oil and heat up a skillet over medium heat. Put the marinated cod fillets in and fry them for 3-4 minutes per side. The flesh should turn opaque if you've got it right. If you have left the skin on, fry the skin sides until it turns crispy then take off the heat. Don't let the skin burn.

Serve:

Serve hot and spoon a healthy serving of the quinoa and broccoli pilaf mixture on to your plate. Add the cod whole or cut into slices. Make crispy, thin toast to give a little crunch to your dinner.

Protein Smoothie
SERVES 1

Prep Time: 25 minutes

Cooking Time: 45 minutes

Nutritional Value per Serving:

Calories: 169

Carbohydrates: 13g

Total Fat: 1g

Protein: 23g

Ingredients

1 small banana

10 oz almond milk

½ cup frozen berries

1 scoop protein powder

Method

Put all the ingredients together in a blender and pulse until a smooth mixture is obtained.

Serve

Pour the prepared smoothie in a glass, top with a few berries, serve and enjoy!

Nutty Berry Quinoa
SERVES 1

Prep Time: 25 minutes

Cooking Time: 45 minutes

Nutritional Value per Serving:

Calories: 178

Carbohydrates: 14g

Total Fat: 5g

Protein: 8g

Ingredients

1 cup almond milk

½ tsp ground cinnamon

1 cup quinoa, rinsed

4 drops stevia

1 cup blueberries, fresh

1 tbsp Earth Balanced Buttery Spread

1 cup strawberries, fresh and sliced

1 cup water

¼ cup raw walnuts, coarsely chopped

Method

Place a saucepan, medium in size, over high heat and then add in the water, quinoa, and almond milk. Bring this concoction to a boil, and then lower the heat to medium and let it simmer. Cover the saucepan with a lid and then let the mixture absorb the liquid, this will take about 15 minutes. Add in the Earth balance along with the stevia extract and stir until well combined. Remove the saucepan from heat and let it cool for minutes, then add in the blueberries, cinnamon and strawberries.

Serve

Pour the quinoa into a serving bowl, top it with walnuts, serve and enjoy with your friends and family.

Chicken Salad Pita
SERVES 4

Prep Time: 25 minutes

Cooking Time: 45 minutes

Nutritional Value per Serving:

Calories: 155

Carbohydrates: 11g

Total Fat: 1.5g

Protein: 6g

Ingredients

1 lb chicken breast, skinless and boneless, cooked and chilled

Add veggies of your choice, if you want

3 celery ribs, large in size, diced into small pieces

Salt and Pepper, for seasoning

Lemon Juice, a few squeezes

1/3 cup onions, diced

4 whole wheat pitas

4 tbsp vegan or organic mayonnaise

Method

Take the chicken breast and slice it into thin long strips, and then chop it into bite-sized dices. Throw these chicken pieces into a mixing bowl and then add in the onion, mayonnaise, celery, pepper, salt, and lemon juice. Taste and adjust the seasoning if required, and then mix it all together to make sure that all the ingredients are thoroughly, and evenly mixed. Take your whole-wheat pitas and then place the prepared chicken mixture over them, after dividing the salad equally.

Serve

Make a sandwich using the pitas and then serve with fresh greens on the side.

Greek Pasta Salad
SERVES 4

Prep Time: 25 minutes

Cooking Time: 45 minutes

Nutritional Value per Serving:

Calories: 153

Carbohydrates: 15g

Total Fat: 1g

Protein: 9g

Ingredients

For the Dressing

4 tbsp olive oil

Salt and Pepper, for seasoning

2 tbsp fresh lemon juice

1 tbsp fresh mint, finely chopped

1 tbsp fresh oregano, finely chopped

For the Salad

8 oz whole-wheat macaroni pasta

1 can of artichoke hearts, 15 oz, with the artichokes drained and halved

1 cucumber, diced into small pieces

20 Greek Kalamata olives, pitted and halved

18 grape tomatoes, quartered

2 tbsp chives, fresh and finely chopped

Method

To make the dressing, combine all of the ingredients in a mixing bowl, and whisk it until well combined. Taste and adjust the seasoning, if required. meanwhile, in a large saucepan filled with water, cook the macaroni as per the instructions given on its packet. Once cooked, drained it and transfer to a mixing bowl, add in the dressing and toss it until all the pieces of macaroni are evenly covered with it. Once the pasta is cool, add in the rest of the ingredients and then mix it together until thoroughly combined.

Serve

Chill the macaroni until it is ready to be served. Serve and enjoy!

Cashew Chicken Salad
SERVES 4

Prep Time: 25 minutes

Cooking Time: 45 minutes

Nutritional Value per Serving:

Calories: 148

Carbohydrates: 9g

Total Fat: 1g

Protein: 7g

Ingredients

2 cups cooked rice noodles

For the Salad

! cup chicken breast, skinless and boneless, cooked and then diced

2 cups Napa Cabbage, shredded

1 scallions, sliced

1 cup carrots, sliced

½ cup red bell pepper, sliced

1 orange, fresh and cut into chunks.

For the Dressing

1 tbsp cashew butter

1 tbsp rice vinegar

2 tbsp lime juice, fresh

For Garnish

1 tbsp cilantro, fresh and finely chopped

3 tbsp cashew nuts, coarsely chopped

Method

Combine all of the ingredients for the dressing and then whisk it together until well mixed. Set aside.

Mix the noodles and then salad ingredients in a large mixing bowl and then combine them until evenly incorporated.

Serve

Add the dressing over the salad, toss to combine evenly and then garnish with cashew nuts and cilantro. Enjoy!

Moroccan Salmon Kabobs
SERVES 4

Prep Time: 25 minutes

Cooking Time: 45 minutes

Nutritional Value per Serving:

Calories: 124

Carbohydrates: 12g

Total Fat: 3g

Protein: 8g

Ingredients

1 lb salmon, diced

Bamboo skewers

2 tbsp Moroccan spice

1 zucchini, diced into small pieces

1 oz grape seed oil

1red onion, finely chopped

2 tbsp Cajun spice

Method

Take a mixing bowl, add in the oil and spices and then whisk this mixture until well combined. Add the salmon in the mixing bowl and then rub the spice and oil mixture on all sides of it. Take a plastics zip lock bag, pour the salmon along with the oil, and spice mixture, into it and let it marinade overnight.

When you are ready to make the kabobs, soak the skewers in water for 30 minutes, and then one by one arrange the salmon and vegetables on the skewers. Once you are done, place them on a hot preheated grill and let them cook until the vegetables are tender.

Serve

Transfer to a serving platter, serve and enjoy with your friends and family.

Crockpot Pepper Steak
SERVES 4

Prep Time: 25 minutes

Cooking Time: 45 minutes

Nutritional Value per Serving:

Calories: 244

Carbohydrates: 22g

Total Fat: 6g

Protein: 12g

Ingredients

1 lb lean round steak, cut into long strips

Brown rice, cooked, (optional)

1 onion, medium in size, diced

2 tbsp low sodium soy sauce

1 red pepper, large, chopped

1 can of tomato paste, 12 oz

1 cup button mushrooms, chopped

1 can of stewed tomatoes, 28 oz

2 garlic cloves, finely chopped

1 cup water

Black pepper

Method

Take a slow cooker, and add all of the ingredients except the rice in it. Combine them until well incorporated and then set the lid in place and allow it to cook on low settings for 8-9 hour.

Serve

Once cooked, serve with hot brown rice. Enjoy with your friends and family.

Ginger Glazed Salmon
SERVES 4

Prep Time: 25 minutes

Cooking Time: 45 minutes

Nutritional Value per Serving:

Calories: 165

Carbohydrates: 12g

Total Fat: 3g

Protein: 11g

Ingredients

1 tbsp lemon juice, fresh

2 salmon fillets, 8 oz each

1 tbsp ginger, finely grated

2 tbsp honey

1 tbsp Dijon mustard

1 tbsp low sodium soy sauce

Method

Take a small mixing bowl, add all of the ingredients except the salmon in it and then combine it together until well mixed. Take a shallow baking dish, pour this mixture in it and then spread it out evenly over the base of the baking dish. Take the salmon fillets, place them in the baking dish and then cost one side of each of the fillets with the mixture then flip them over and repeat the same process with the other side. Let them marinade for 30 minutes, turning them every few minutes. Cook the salmon fillets on each side for 4-6 minutes.

Serve

Once cooked, sliced the salmon fillets in half, transfer them to serving platter, serve and enjoy!

Ginger Glazed Sweet Peppers
SERVES 2

Prep Time: 25 minutes

Cooking Time: 45 minutes

Nutritional Value per Serving:

Calories: 67

Carbohydrates: 4g

Total Fat: 1g

Protein: 2g

Ingredients

2 large bell peppers, mix of different colors,

2 tbsp ginger, fresh and finely chopped

2 tbsp coconut oil

Salt and Pepper for seasoning

1 clove of garlic, large, finely chopped

Method

Wash the peppers and cut them along the centre. Trim the top along with the stem end and then slice of the bottom as well, get rid of the seeds, and then slice the peppers into thin long strips. Place a sauté pan over medium low heat, add in the oil, and then add the pepper strips and cook them until they become soft. Make sure to stir all the while, to prevent them from burning. Add the ginger and garlic and stir to make sure that they are evenly coated. Cook for another two minutes and then take them out.

Serve

Try them out and enjoy them with any other dish of your choice.

Rosemary Chicken
SERVES 2

Prep Time: 25 minutes

Cooking Time: 45 minutes

Nutritional Value per Serving:

Calories: 223

Carbohydrates: 18g

Total Fat: 7g

Protein: 9g

Ingredients

2 chicken breasts, skinless and boneless

¼ tsp pepper

1 tbsp rosemary, fresh and finely chopped

½ tsp salt

3 cloves of garlic, finely chopped

2 tbsp red wine vinegar

½ tsp honey

1 tbsp grape seed oil

1 tsp sage, fresh and finely chopped

Method

Take a medium mixing bowl, add in the sage, rosemary, grape seed oil, garlic, pepper, salt, honey and vinegar, and mix it together until well combined. Add in the chicken and coat all of its sides with the prepared mixture. Cover the bowl with cling wrap and allow the chicken to marinade for 24 hours. Place the mixing bowl with the chicken and marinade in the refrigerator during this time. Once you are ready to cook, take it out of the refrigerator, and allow it to reach room temperature then transfer to a preheated grill over medium heat. Cook the chicken for 8-10 minutes per side.

Serve

Once the chicken is cooked, transfer it to a serving platter and then serve it with greens on the side. Enjoy!

Lemon Pepper Halibut
SERVES 4

Prep Time: 25 minutes

Cooking Time: 45 minutes

Nutritional Value per Serving:

Calories: 160

Carbohydrates: 16g

Total Fat: 5g

Protein: 8g

Ingredients

Salty, as required

4 halibut fillets, 6 oz each

3 tbsp olive oil

Lemon pepper for seasoning

4 cups arugula

3 cloves of garlic, finely chopped

¼ cup basil

½ cup sundried tomatoes

¼ cup red wine vinegar

Method

Add the garlic, basil, and tomatoes in a blender and pulse until a smooth mixture is obtained. Add in water and a tablespoon of olive oil and then blend again until well incorporated. Season with salt, then taste and adjust the seasoning as required, and then set aside. Take a piece of halibut, brush it with the remaining olive oil, and sprinkle it with salt and lemon pepper. Place the piece of halibut in a baking dish and repeat the process with the remaining fillets. Once they are all assembled in the baking dish, transfer the dish in a preheated oven at 400oF and allow it to bake for 20-30 minutes or until the fish easily flakes with a fork.

Serve

To serve, place the arugula and sundried tomatoes mixture on a serving platter, place the halibut fillet over it, serve and enjoy!

Golden Chicken Cutlets
SERVES 4

Prep Time: 25 minutes

Cooking Time: 45 minutes

Nutritional Value per Serving:

Calories: 198

Carbohydrates: 11g

Total Fat: 6g

Protein: 7g

Ingredients

1 ½ lb chicken, skinless and boneless

Salt and pepper, for seasoning

1 tsp garlic, finely chopped

½ cup whole wheat flour

2 tbsp olive oil

Method

Cut the chicken breasts into half, lengthwise, and then season both sides generously with pepper and salt. Add the garlic and then rub it evenly on all sides of the chicken. Sprinkle all sides of the chicken with a little bit if flour and then lightly coat all sides with it. Tap lightly against the palm of your hand to get rid of the excess flour and then set aside. Follow the same procedure with the remaining chicken. Place a pan over medium heat, along with the olive oil, and allow it to heat up until sizzling hot. Then add the chicken cutlets into the pan, and cook them until they are golden brown in color from all sides. Once the chicken is cooked from all sides, remove than pan from heat.

Serve

Transfer the chicken onto a serving platter, serve hot and enjoy with your friends and family.

Asian Chicken Lettuce Cups
SERVES 4

Prep Time: 25 minutes

Cooking Time: 45 minutes

Nutritional Value per Serving:

Calories: 154

Carbohydrates: 14g

Total Fat: 7g

Protein: 9g

Ingredients

2 tbsp black sesame seeds

½ cup snow peas

½ cup scallions, sliced finely

2 cups chicken, boneless and skinless, cooked and shredded

Iceberg Lettuce

½ cup red bell pepper, sliced finely

Tahini dressing

½ cup carrots, sliced finely

For the Tahini Dressing

¼ cup tahini, ½ cup light sesame oil

1 tsp garlic, finely chopped

¼ tsp Thai Kitchen Red Chili Paste

4 tsp lemon juice, freshly squeezed

4 tsp low sodium soy sauce

1 ½ tsp dark sesame oil

¼ tsp ginger, fresh and finely chopped

¼ tsp salt

Method

Mix all the ingredients for the tahini dressing and set aside. Take a large pan filled with water, add a little bit of salt in it, about ½ a teaspoon and then add in the peas in it to boil. Allow the peas to boil for 30 seconds and then drain them. Transfer the peas into a large bowl, add in the rest of the ingredients except the lettuce cups in it along with the dressing, and combined them until well incorporated. Scoop this mixture into iceberg lettuce cups and then sprinkle a little bit of sesame seeds over it.

Serve

Transfer the prepared lettuce cups onto a serving platter, serve and enjoy!

Italian Style Chicken Fingers
SERVES 4

Prep Time: 25 minutes

Cooking Time: 45 minutes

Nutritional Value per Serving:

Calories: 165

Carbohydrates: 24g

Total Fat: 6g

Protein: 13g

Ingredients

½ cup Italian spiced whole wheat

1 tsp grape seed oil

1 ½ cup marinara pasta sauce

1 lb chicken tenders, skinless and boneless

Method

Take a large mixing bowl add in the Italian spiced whole wheat in it and then coat the chicken with this mixture. Transfer the chicken on a baking sheet lined with parchment paper, and then repeat the same procedure with the remaining pieces of chicken. Transfer the baking sheet in a preheated oven with its temperature set at 450oF and allow the chicken to bake for 15-20 minutes, making sure to turn it once during the time, to allow it to cook evenly. Meanwhile, heat the marinara sauce in a small saucepan placed over low heat.

Serve

Once the chicken tenders are cooked, take them out of the oven, transfer to a serving platter, top with the marinara sauce, and serve with a vegetable salad on the side. Enjoy!

End Note

Keeping in mind, that the Daniel Diet is meant to embody a biblical way of leading your life we've made sure to include recipes that are easy to make and completely nutritious which will enable you to fast easily without suffering from any hunger pangs throughout your work day.

Food and your spiritual self share your body in common and that is the temple where both come together. With the help of these recipes, you'll be able to keep yourself feeling fit, healthy and hereby, maintain the precious temple for your spiritual self to enjoy and when you feel good from the inside, you don't just look good, you glow from the inside out.

To make sure that at the end of a fast, you don't feel weak; these brilliant recipes leave your feeling good and rejuvenated. By following the plan, you will be able to lead a healthy life, which is based on spiritual and physical aspects of life.

The recipes are not hard and fast and you can play around with them as much as you like if you want to substitute one particular ingredient for another. You can choose to have them before you start your fast or choose to have them afterwards as well.

In this book, you will find Daniel Diet recipes, which are healthy, tasty, and full of nutrition. In the end, we wish you a good spiritual journey ahead.

Happy Cooking!

Made in the USA
Columbia, SC
24 September 2023